TRICK OR TREAT?

Annie and Jason, a pair of twins, aren't that happy when Mum sends them off to stay with an aunt they've never even met before for their birthday. Aunt May turns out to be OK, but John, who looks after her, is definitely weird and a little sinister. The twins begin to feel very uneasy and even more so when they discover that someone is trying to murder their aunt. They have a pretty good idea who it is and are determined to foil him at all costs, but they soon find they've taken on more than they bargained for and get a rather unexpected birthday surprise . . .

Thriller Firsts is an exciting series of fast-paced adventure stories expecially for younger readers of the seven to nine age group. With clear, straightforward text and plenty of illustrations they are ideal for every child who loves a good, gripping read.

Jon Blake was born in Berkshire in 1954 and was brought up in Southampton. After getting a degree from York University he taught for a while as well as working for a time both as a furniture salesman and a community centre warden. His first novel, *Yatesy's Rap* was published in 1984. This is his first book for Blackie.

Other titles in the series

The Creature in the Dark   Robert Westall
The Raft   Alison Morgan
Jumping Jack   David Wiseman

Illustrated by Caroline Ewen

Blackie

Copyright © 1988 Jon Blake
Illustrations © 1988 Caroline Ewen
First Published 1988 by Blackie and Son Ltd

Cover illustration by Caroline Ewen

All rights reserved. No part of this publication may be reproduced, stored in a retrieval system, or transmitted in any form or by any means, electronic, mechanical, photocopying, recording or otherwise without the written permission of the Publishers.

British Library Cataloguing in Publication Data

Blake, Jon
Trick or Treat?—(Thriller firsts).
I. Title II. Ewen, Caroline III. Series
823'.914 [J]   PZ7

ISBN 0-216-92428-6

Blackie and Son Ltd
7 Leicester Place
London WC2H 7BP

Typesetting by Jamesway Graphics, Middleton, Manchester
Printed in Great Britain by Thomson Litho Ltd, East Kilbride, Scotland

The wardrobe's moving.

It creeps towards me, half an inch, then an inch. It groans, it rattles, and it gives out a big old creak. Its door shakes, then bursts open. Annie jumps out.

'I told you!' she says. 'There's nothing in there.'

I flop back on Mum's bed and think again.

'I know!' I go. 'Under the floorboards!' Annie pulls up the corner of the carpet. 'It's concrete,' she says. 'We ain't got no floorboards.'

'You don't think . . . she's forgot?' I say.

'Don't be stupid!' says Annie. 'How could Mum forget *our birthday*?'

I'm not so sure. We've been under the beds, on top of the bookcase, and inside the airing cupboard. We've emptied the drawers and we've rattled the cake tins. I swear there's no presents in this flat.

'She's got us gift tokens again,' I go.

'I don't want gift tokens!' says Annie. 'I want a present. I want a *surprise*!'

Annie checks under the bed again. The front door goes. We rush back into the living room and sit on the sofa, two little angels. Mum lumbers in with the shopping, three bags. She's fit to drop.

'What have you two been up to?' she says, taking one look at us.

'Nothing, Mum! Why?'

Mum looks around to see what's broken, or stained, or missing. Then she kicks off her shoes and flops down in the chair. We take a good hard look at the bulges in the Co-op bags.

I'm not sure how poor we are but I think we're getting poorer. Today we have baked potatoes for tea and that makes three times this week. Mum used to get money off the DHSS but I think that's stopped, and now I don't know where she gets money from. She's trying to take her A-levels so she can go up in the world, but something always gets in the way and she never does the exam. She is getting more and more moody.

'Jason!' she says. 'If I've told you once I've told you a thousand times! Don't play football indoors! I can't afford another window broken!'

I kick my football under the sofa. Mum says she wants a word with the two of us.

'I'm taking my exam in two weeks,' she says. 'I've got to have some peace and quiet. You two are going away for a while.'

'Oh, Mum!'

'Don't start. I've already made the plans, so there's no arguing about it.'

'We ain't going to Dad's!'

'Ssh! You're staying with your Aunt May.'

'Aunt May? Who's she?'

'She's your great-aunt really. She remembers you well enough, in your pram. I'm taking you down to see her tomorrow, then I'll pick you up on Sunday.'

'Sunday? But Sunday's our birthday!'

'Ssh! I know it's your birthday, don't worry!'

'But what about our —?'

I'm just going to say 'presents', but I shut up quick. Who knows, we may get nothing at all.

Next morning we pack some things and set off for the train station with Mum. It's cold, with a gloomy grey sky, and the buses are all squashed full of people expecting rain. I wear my hand-me-down duffle coat with 'A.N. Gardner' printed in the back. I don't know who 'A.N. Gardner' is. I hope I never have an accident or they might send me back to the wrong house.

The train station's called 'Bristol Parkway' and it's boring. Mum uses her Family Railcard. We buy a triple-decker sandwich and catch a train for South Wales.

'Your Aunt May lives in Barry Island,' says Mum.

'Have we got to get a boat?' says Annie.

'Oh, no!' says Mum. 'It's not really an island.'

We go down a tunnel right under the River Severn. Mum buys a cup of tea with a round tea-bag in. Everything's very strange today.

At last we get there. As we come out of the station we can smell the sea. But there's not a soul in sight. The shops are boarded up and the street's full of litter. We walk past a funfair, but there are no lights on it, and the rides and roundabouts loom up like metal ghosts. No one comes to the seaside in October.

Mum looks anxious.

'I thought she might be here to meet us,' she says.

'What's she look like?' I go.

'Look for a wheelchair,' says Mum.

'There!' says Annie. 'Is that her?' She points down to the seafront. There's a big concrete arcade down there, with crumbling pillars like an old temple. I can just make out a grey head and a shawl and a wheelchair. It's all alone, facing the cold sea and the crying seagulls.

'That's her,' says Mum. 'Whatever's she

doing down there?'

Mum runs us down to the arcade, calling 'May!' As we get closer, the old lady struggles to turn her head. She must be ninety. The lines on her face are deep and there are dark circles round her eyes. She looks shocked.

'Susan!' she says. 'My goodness, what's the time? John! John! Oh, where's he got to now?'

Mum tries to calm her down. Mum says

we've had a good journey and what matters is that we're here. Aunt May asks if we're really Jason and Annie, and says how much we've changed since we were two. She gets us to come closer and looks us up and down, beaming all over her face.

'Don't you remember your old Aunt May?' she says.

We shake our heads. Mum ruffles our hair, tidies our jackets, and tells us to be good, and remember Aunt May is an old lady and can't run around clearing up after us. Then she says goodbye, because she's got to get the next train back. I watch her get smaller and smaller, and for a second I really think I'll run after her, except I'd look so stupid.

So there we are, in the middle of nowhere, left with someone we don't even know.

'Ah!' says Aunt May. 'There he is! John! John!'

Suddenly a man appears, climbing over the concrete wall to the beach. He's tall, a bit fat, in jeans and a smart leather jacket. His hair is short, tinted, and combed back. When he sees

us he looks uncomfortable and talks to Aunt May as if we're not there.

'Still here, then?' he says to her.

'Well, of course I am! I'm not going far without you pushing, am I?'

'These the twins, are they?' he says, still not looking at us.

'Yes. We missed them at the station, thanks to you.'

'That's a shame, isn't it?' he says, with a little smile that makes my insides go cold.

Aunt May's house is a few minutes' walk up

the hill from the beach, past a boating-lake and a park. There's a lawn at the front and French windows into the living room. French windows are like glass doors, and Aunt May tells us they cost her a fortune.

John has got the keys, and lets us into the house. He seems to be in control of everything, and I suppose he must be a relative. Aunt May hasn't said. Perhaps she thinks we know who he is.

The house has an old smell. We go into the front room, the room with the French windows. It looks like a museum. There's a big black dresser down one wall, covered in photographs, and an owl in a glass case. In front of that is this weird sofa with only one arm. Aunt May has her own chair, by the gas fire. She sits there and we sit on the sofa, which is hard. John pulls the curtains in front of the windows, checks the grandfather clock in the corner of the room, and goes to light the gas fire with a match.

'Oh, I hate that fire!' says Aunt May.

'It's all right,' says John.

'I'm never sure if it's on or off,' says Aunt

May. 'I'm scared the gas is going to come out in the night.'

John lets out a deep breath.

'What do you want me to do?' he says. 'Take it all apart again and check it? There's absolutely nothing wrong with it. The only way gas is going to come out is if someone turns it on.'

Aunt May's still doubtful, but John looks like he might lose his temper.

'Very well,' says Aunt May, 'I'll take your word for it.'

John lights the fire. There's a little flash, then it's working. The flash makes me jump a bit, and I hope no one notices. I don't like Aunt May's room at all, especially that owl behind me.

'Now, children,' says Aunt May. 'Would you like to take some books up to your room?'

Annie and me look at each other. We don't like books much, except comic books, but we're scared of being rude.

'Take your pick!' says Aunt May, reaching up and opening her bookcase.

We get up and go to the bookcase. Aunt May says she hopes we aren't like those children who watch TV all the time, and tells us she threw out her TV the day ITV started, with those foolish adverts.

'There's just too much nonsense in people's heads these days,' she says.

I read along the rows of books, looking for something with pictures. The first book's called *The Terrors of St Mary's* by Maria Rose. The second's called *Bunty's Midnight Feast* by Maria Rose. The third is called *Haunted Holiday* by Maria Rose. In fact just about every book is by Maria Rose. She must be the most famous writer in the world. Not that I've ever heard of her.

Annie picks out *Oh, No, It's Gassy Cooke!* by Maria Rose, and opens the mouldy yellow pages, not looking happy. Aunt May beams at her.

'I think you'll like that one!' she says. 'It's a bit spicy, that one!'

Annie takes the book back to the sofa.

'I know what you're thinking,' Aunt May says to me.

I quickly turn my back to her, in case she really does know.

'You're thinking they're all girls' books, aren't you, dear?' she says.

'Mmm,' I mumble.

'I know these days there's no difference between you children,' says Aunt May. 'But in *my* day . . . well, never mind. I'll tell you what, Jason. If you pick out one of those books and read it tonight, I'll let you play with what's under my chair. Is that fair?'

'Mmm,' I mumble.

'Very well.'

Aunt May reaches under her chair and brings out a white china potty.

'Oh, no!' she says. 'That's not it.'

John moves towards her.

'No, no, I can manage,' says Aunt May.

She fishes around under the chair and brings out a brand new football. She hands it to me.

'Thank you!' I go.

'Aren't you forgetting something?' says Aunt May.

'Oh, yeah!'

I pick out the nearest book, *Haunted Holiday*. Annie's sulking. At home we always get exactly the same things.

'He's broken three windows at home!' she mumbles.

'Has he?' says Aunt May. 'Well, I'm sure he'll be more careful here, won't you, Jason?'

I hug my football in one arm and my book in another and tell her I'll be really really careful. Then I look at Annie as if to say 'So there!' Aunt May decides it's time we went up to our room, and John shows us the way.

Our room's on the top floor. It's got one tiny window and a sloping ceiling. It smells musty, like it hasn't been used for fifty years. There's an old-fashioned dressing-table and two small beds. On the dressing-table is a big pottery bowl with a painted jug standing inside it. Round the walls are pictures of flowers which look like they've been cut from chocolate boxes. The wallpaper's faded and the curtains are covered in more flowers—strange, ugly flowers that I don't like looking at.

John tells us to unpack our things and come

down for dinner in half an hour. When I drop the football he traps it and passes it back, so he may be all right after all.

'I want to go home!' says Annie, soon as he's gone.

'Don't be so wet!' I go. 'It's all right here.'

I fold my book open at page fifty to make it look like I've been reading it, then give my ball another boot. It bounces off the wall, rattles the dressing-table, and just misses the window.

For dinner we get trout, which is a fish I've never seen before. I get more than Annie. John dishes everything up, then takes the bones out of Aunt May's trout. He's got a wicked knife, razor sharp. Aunt May holds her head back as he uses it, and her hands come up off the table like she's nervous. But John knows how to use it. When he's finished, he wipes along the blade with a serviette. Then he checks it up against the light, and lays it carefully next to his plate. I ask if I can look at it and he says I must be joking.

'Goodness me!' says Aunt May, after we've

finished our ice-cream. 'Nine o'clock. Time for you two to get to bed.'

My record latest night is one o'clock and Mum usually lets us stay up till News at Ten, but I haven't been to bed at nine since I was six.

I lie awake in the starchy white sheets and watch the wind suck and blow the curtains. The seagulls are crying and Annie's snuffling into her pillow.

'What's the matter with you?' I go.

'I don't like it here,' she says. 'I don't like that man.'

'What? John? Why not?'

'He never looks at you properly. There's something funny about him. I want to go home.'

'You're just imagining things.'

I turn over and watch the curtains again. It makes me feel dead brave, telling Annie not to feel scared. But after staring at those ugly painted flowers for a while, I start imagining things too. I see faces in the flowers, all blown up and twisted and staring back at me. I can feel nightmares coming on.

Suddenly Annie sits bolt upright in bed. 'What's that?' she says.

My heart starts to bang. 'What?' I go.

'That noise!'

'You're imagining things.'

'Listen!'

'Huh!' I go, but I listen all the same. And then I begin to hear it. It's a rumbling, far away. I sit up. The rumbling goes on. Somehow it seems to come through the floor, not through the window. It's inside this house.

'What is it?' says Annie

'How do I know?'

'Jason, turn the landing light on!.'

I move slowly out of bed. I crawl between the black shadow of the dressing-table and the flickering faces on the curtains. Everything's ready to reach out and grab me. I reach the door and put my hand round the cold handle. I'm sure that when I open it a great cloud of bats is going to come flapping into the room.

Suddenly something's on me. It's got me by the pyjama bottoms. My heart stops and

I thrash away with my hands in the blackness.

'Stop it!' it goes.

It's Annie. She's come after me.

'Stupid!' I go.

'Thought you weren't scared!' says Annie.

Slowly I open the door. It's OK. We crawl out on our hands and knees. I'm scared my fingers are going to land on a spider, or a big moth, or a rat's tail. The rumbling's louder.

'Jason! Find the light!'

My hands scramble over the walls. I can't find the switch. Perhaps there isn't a switch.

Click! Light.

'Jason!' says Annie.

'What?'

'You're all white!''

'So? So are you!'

'Ssh!'

We listen hard. The rumbling's coming from downstairs. But there's something else as well. It's a voice. But it's not normal. It sounds . . . frightened.

We creep to the top of the stairs.

'I think it's coming from her room,' I go.

Annie starts off down the stairs. I grab hold of her arm.

'Where are you going?' I go.

'We've got to find out what it is,' says Annie.

'Why?'

'Come on, we've got to!'

Annie's eyes are open wide, staring. She watches horror films from under a cushion but she's still got to watch them. Something draws her to them, and now it's drawing her down the stairs towards that voice.

'It's Aunt May!' she whispers.

'Who's she talking to?'

'I think she's talking to herself.'

We step off the last creaky stair into the downstairs hall. A crack of light's shining under Aunt May's door. Annie grabs my sleeve and her hand's trembling. We come up close to the door and listen but we can't make it out for that rumbling noise.

'Let's go back up,' I go.

'No!' says Annie. 'Wait!'

Suddenly the rumbling stops. At the same instant we hear Aunt May's voice, loud and

clear. It turns my insides to jelly.

'He's going to kill me!' she says. 'Don't they realize? He's going to kill me!'

We fly for the stairs in a blind panic. And as we scramble madly for the top, the basement door swings open and John's face stares up at us.

When I wake up next morning I'm in all my clothes and the dressing-table is pushed up against the door. I start to remember what happened, but it's all mixed up with my bad dreams. John didn't really creep into the room carrying his knife, and there wasn't really a fight, and I didn't really kill him. But Aunt May's voice—that was real, and that was why we couldn't go to sleep.

I think it's early. It's very quiet out, and there's a mist across the front lawn. I shake Annie. Her eyes open, all red from tiredness or crying or both. She sits up and looks around the room, as if she's forgotten it.

'I want to go home!' she says.

'I know,' I go. 'Let's creep out and ring Mum.'

'What if he hears us?'

'We'll tell him we're getting the milk in.'

We put on our plimsolls and tiptoe down, hardly daring to breath. I take a quick look at the basement door. Closed. We open the front door like we're cracking a safe, and slip outside. The lawn's frosty and our feet make a soft crunch as they creep over it. Then we reach the road and leg it.

'Where's the phone?' I hiss at Annie.

'In a phone box!'' she says.

I race down towards the beach, terrified a long arm's going to stretch out of the house and grab my neck, no matter how far I get. One or two cars go by. I want to chase them and knock on their windows, but Mum said never to talk to strangers.

At last we find a phone box. We argue over how to use it and fight for the phone. INSERT MONEY NOW flashes up, and we suddenly realize we've not got any ready. I fumble through my pockets for 10p, looking back up the road every five seconds. Annie finds her address book and reads out the number in a squeaky voice. We fight to tap it out between

us and end up getting it all wrong. I bring my fist up.

'Don't you hit me!' says Annie.

'Well, get out the way!'

'Remember what Mum said!'

I punch the side of the phone box and end up in agony, sucking my fist.

Annie taps out the number. We both listen.

'Hello?' someone says.

'Mum?' we both go.

'Who's that?' says the voice.

'Jason!' I go.

'Annie!' says Annie.

'Who?' says the voice. 'Geoffrey?'

I get an awful feeling. 'Is that you, Mum?' I go.

'I think you've got the wrong number,' says the voice.

I glare at Annie. She looks at her book.

'Is that five three two two eight?' she says.

'Yes,' says the voice.

'Can we speak to Mum, please?' says Annie.

'Look,' says the voice. 'I don't know who you are, but you've just got me out of bed. Is this some kind of stupid trick or what?'

'Where's our mum?' says Annie.

'Kids!' shouts the voice. 'Stupid kids! I've got this phone tapped, you know! I'll have the law on you!'

Annie puts down the phone. 'What's going on?' she says to me, as if I could answer.

There's an empty promenade beside the beach, and at the end of it a little grassy hill. When you walk up the hill you find yourself on a patch of grass going out towards the sea, with steep edges and big slabs of rock like slices of cake slipping into the ocean. We walk to the very end of this patch of grass and sit with our feet hanging over. The sea's grey and huge like a great heaving soup. Annie gazes at it the same way she gazes at Aunt May's door and horror films. It's so vast and terrifying sometimes you think it would be better to dive in and let it swallow you up. I imagine doing it. Then I imagine what it feels like to hit the freezing water and suddenly be struggling for your life. I don't like to even think about that.

'Why should he want to kill her anyway?' I say, suddenly.

'How do I know?' says Annie. 'Perhaps she's rich.'

'Why doesn't she live in a bigger house then?'

'Perhaps she doesn't want to spend it. Perhaps it's under a mattress or something.'

'That only happens in stories.'

'Maybe we're in a story.'

'Eh? You're weird, you are.'

Annie grabs my arm and tells me to be quiet. I look back over my shoulder and there's John, coming for us. There's no way out, so I smile and say hello, dead friendly.

'What are you two doing?' he says. 'Picking mushrooms?'

'No!' I go. 'Honest!'

John bears down closer. 'Keep your hair on,' he says. 'I'm only joking.'

I feel around behind me. My fingers close round a jagged piece of rock. John comes right up, towering over us like the Incredible Hulk against the sky. His eyes focus on us like we're something at the end of a microscope. They're very sharp.

'What's that you've got in your hand?' he says.

I slowly bring my hand from behind my back. I unfold my fingers and look carefully at the piece of rock.

'Found an interesting stone,' I go.

'Oh, yeah?' says John, squatting down. 'Interested in stones, are you?'

'Yes, very,' I go.

'Let's have a look then.'

I pass him the piece of rock. He turns it over in his hand, checking every detail with his sharp eyes. Then he reaches in his pocket and pulls out a little hammer. Tap! The rock splits clean in two. He holds one half up to me.

'Ever seen a fossil before?' he says.

We both shake our heads. John passes the half-stone under our eyes. There's a shell-shape in it.

'Now you see that?' he says. 'That's a fossil. That was alive once, that creature. Now it's turned to stone.'

John watches our faces, staying very still, as if it was him that was turned to stone. He tells us a long story of how the fossil was made, and

how many centuries it took. He talks about sand and sea and rocks and fire, and how long the life on Earth has been going, and what tiny specks we are, and how short our lives are, really.

'Shame, eh?' he says.

We get interested. John breaks some more rocks. When he doesn't find a fossil he flings the rock into the sea and makes it bounce. One rock bounces seven times. He teaches me how to bounce rocks, but Annie doesn't want to. She wanders off while John gets hold of my arm and guides it till I can make a rock bounce four times. It's ace!

'Excuse me,' I go, 'but who are you?'

'Who am I?' he says. 'I'm the King of China, Sunshine!'

'No, who are you really?' I go. 'Are you a relative?'

'I'm someone's relative, aren't I?' he says.

I want to ask him more questions, but he suddenly decides it's time to get back for breakfast. He calls Annie and starts wandering back. Then he seems to have second thoughts. He gets us together and his voice goes quiet.

'Listen, kids,' he says. 'There's something you ought to know about your aunt, right?'

'What?'

'Put it this way. She ain't quite all there. She gets some funny idea in her head, and she just won't listen to reason. Like that gas fire. You can't tell her.'

'What?' I go. 'You mean she just . . . imagines things?'

'Too right she does. All kinds of things. I should take what she says with a pinch of salt if I were you.'

I nod. Why didn't I think of that? It's obvious! She's an old lady! I'm that happy I run all the way back, like I've just come out the dentist's with no fillings.

During the next couple of days I go back to the beach to collect more fossils. Annie spends most of her time locked away, and so does Aunt May. Annie's reading her book and I don't know what Aunt May's doing. John comes out sometimes and even plays football with me. He teaches me how to do in-swingers and out-swingers and how to block-tackle, except his legs are so strong I just fall over when I try to get the ball off him. I'm sure he must be in a team but when I ask him he says he plays for the Washington Sky-Blue Pinks in the Blind League.

When I get to bed I'm so knacked out I go straight off to sleep, so I forget about the noises in the night and the faces in the curtains. Annie says she can still hear the rumbling, but I'm getting fed up of her and I take no notice.

One afternoon Annie helps Aunt May clean the silver. Afterwards Annie looks very bothered about something.

'What's up with you?' I go, balancing my football on my foot.

'I don't think there's anything wrong with Aunt May,' says Annie.

'Just 'cos you like her!'

'It ain't 'cos I like her. I just been talking to her all afternoon, and she never said anything stupid.'

'Why's she keep that owl then?'

'How do I know? It's just the way she was brought up, I suppose. Anyway, why should we believe that John and not her?'

'Just 'cos you don't like him.'

'I don't *trust* him!'

'All right, then. What you gonna do about it?'

Annie thinks for a while, and I block-tackle the dressing-table.

'I know,' she says. 'We'll test her out. We'll see if her mind really is wandering.'

Next day we knock on Aunt May's door. She tells us to wait and about two minutes later she opens it.

'Come and look, Aunt May!' says Annie. 'We've just seen something really *weird*!'

'What's this?' says Aunt May, looking confused.

'Come and look, Auntie!'

Annie grabs at Aunt May's arm and starts dragging her down the hall. Aunt May hobbles as well as she can. We get to the kitchen.

'In here, Auntie!' says Annie. 'We turned on the tap just now, and all these little fishes came out!'

'Are you sure?' says Aunt May.

'They're in the sink! Come and look!'

Aunt May struggles over to the sink. Annie jumps up and down, pointing.

'There!' she goes. 'Look, it's full of them.'

Aunt May peers over the edge, then hobbles back to face us, looking puzzled.

'Can't you see them, Aunt May?' says Annie.

Aunt May looks again.

'You *must* be able to see them!' says Annie. 'There's thousands of them!'

'Are they very small?' says Aunt May.

'No, they're about an inch long. They just came out the tap, Auntie!'

Aunt May feels in the pocket of her cardigan and brings out her glasses. She tries again. But she still can't seem to see those fishes. When she turns back again, her eyes flash from Annie to me and back again, like a hawk's eyes.

'Do you know what I think?' she says.

'No,' says Annie.

'I think they were flying fishes!' says Aunt May. 'I think they've flown away.'

Aunt May gives us a long, slow wink.

'Honestly!' says Annie. 'They were there, weren't they, Jason?'

'Yeah!' I go, a bit weakly.

Aunt May folds her arms. 'I'll tell you what I *can* see,' she says.

'What's that?' says Annie, nervously.

'I can see two very naughty children,' says Aunt May, 'trying to put one over their old auntie!'

Aunt May draws us closer and holds up a warning finger. Then she recites to us:

'A wise old owl sat on an oak.
The more she heard, the less she spoke.
The less she spoke, the more she heard.
Now wasn't that a wise old bird?'

That night I have a dream. I'm in a car, but I can't drive. I'm going downhill, out of control, screaming round corners, flying over traffic lights. I know I'm going to crash. I think that if I relax and just don't care, it won't matter. Then I fly off the edge of a cliff, and hear someone say 'He's dead!' Except I'm not in the car, I'm watching. Suddenly I panic. I fight to get my eyes open, but they're stuck fast. I fight and fight and at last I force them open. I'm staring straight at Annie.

'Jason!' she says. 'Wake up! It's started again!'

I jerk myself up. I feel sick. The faces in the flowers stare back at me.

'Listen, Jason! The rumbling!'

Sure enough, there it is again. It's no good hiding under the pillow.

'Come on, Jason!'

Annie feels her way to the door. I follow, heart thudding. We click on the landing light and begin the long creep downstairs. The crack of light shines out from under Aunt May's door. Annie presses her ear to the keyhole.

'Is the rumbling in there?' I whisper.

'No,' she says.

'Is she talking?'

'I don't think so.'

Annie moves away from the door. 'That noise!' she says. 'It's coming from below.'

'I ain't going down the basement!'

'Let's just try the door.'

'No!'

I grab her arm, but she pulls away and feels down the wall to the basement door.

'Yes!' she whispers. 'It's down here! It's down here, Jason!'

Annie takes hold of the handle.

'No!' I whisper. The door clicks open. The rumbling comes up loud and light flashes into our eyes. Suddenly Aunt May begins to talk, fast and frightened. Annie pulls the basement door shut and we race back down the corridor. This time there's no mistaking what she's saying:

'They think I'm mad! That man has got to their minds! And now he means to kill me! On *their birthday*! I have till Sunday night on this Earth!'

I don't think Annie slept at all that night. When I went to sleep she was still curled up in the corner of the room, sucking her thumb and turning through the pages of her book. I don't know how many times I told her it would be all right, but every time I said it it sounded less convincing.

When I wake up she's still there, head nodding, looking exhausted. I reach for the calendar and look at the date. Saturday. Tomorrow's the day we look forward to all year.

'Jason', Annie mumbles, soon as she sees me, 'there's something funny about this book.'

'What d'you mean?'

'It's got a woman in it . . . and she's just like Mum.'

I go cold inside. 'You been dreaming!' I go.

'No,' says Annie. 'Listen.'

Annie pulls the book upwards like it's some huge weight, and starts reading: ' "Mrs Davies lived in Bristol. She was five feet four with warm brown eyes and rather too many grey hairs for her age." '

'So?' I go. 'That could be anyone.'

'Listen, Jason! "One thing she could not leave alone was rice pudding. She would eat one bowlful after another, always with a spoonful of jam, and a generous sprinkling of nutmeg." '

'Everyone has rice pudding like that.'

'Listen! "Her favourite place to eat rice pudding . . . was *in the bath*!" '

'Mum!' I go.

'Of course it is!' says Annie

I start to pull on my clothes. 'But how come?' I go.

'I don't know', says Annie. 'Maybe the book is some kind of . . . clue.'

'Have you read it all? It might explain what's going on.'

Annie shakes her head. 'I've thought of that,' she says. 'But the trouble is, every sentence could be a clue. Every word could be. It's impossible to know. Except . . . there is one thing.'

'What?'

'In chapter three there's an escaped criminal,' says Annie, moving closer.

'So?'

'He lives in a basement.'

Just as she says it there's a loud slam. We rush to the window, just in time to see Aunt May in her wheelchair and John pushing. They disappear up the road. For the first time, we're in the house alone.

'This is it,' says Annie. 'This is our chance.'

'They might be just posting a letter!'

'Come *on*, Jason!'

I check out of the window again. Then we clatter down the stairs. Even though we know no one's in the house, we slow down when we reach Aunt May's door and Annie puts a finger to her lips. She tries the handle, but the door's locked.

And now for the basement.

I keep a watch on the front door. I hear Annie hiss 'It's open!' I turn to see her disappearing down the stone steps and into God-knows-what.

The basement smells like a church — a smell of damp stones and cold and moss. I creep downwards feeling like a criminal. At the bottom of the steps we find a purple moth-eaten curtain. Slowly we peel it back, till at last we're face to face with John's secret room.

At first nothing seems too strange about it, except the shelves seem to belong to a garden shed, with potting compost, rusty tools, and an old bike lamp. It's about the size of our bedroom at home, with a single bed, a rail for hanging clothes, and an old office desk. There's no window, just a metal grille high up on the wall, letting in light in dim stripes. All over the desk, the chairs and the floor are sheets of paper, some plain, some typed on.

His clothes are on a chair and there's a drawing of a woman with no clothes on up on the wall. I don't suppose anyone else has ever been down here.

'There's nothing here,' I go. 'Let's go back.'

'No, wait!' says Annie. 'What's that?' She points to a strange tall basket in the corner. It looks like the baskets that snakes come out of. Annie edges over, reaches out one hand, and whips off the lid.

'Pooh!' she says. 'It's his dirty clothes!' Back goes the lid, quick.

'You don't even know what you're looking for,' I whisper.

'Ssh!' says Annie. She goes to the desk and tries the drawers. She doesn't care! She's a criminal!

'That's funny,' she says, pulling out a sock.

'What is?'

'None of these socks make a pair.'

'Perhaps he puts them on his head, for robberies.'

'That's stockings, stupid!'

Annie clears a sleeping-bag, and suddenly jumps back towards me. 'Oh, my God!' she squeals. 'It's a coffin!'

I push her aside. 'That ain't a coffin!' I go. 'That's a blanket-box! Even you couldn't fit in that.'

'Don't say that!'

I check the top of the desk. A typewriter, a tape recorder, and that little hammer of his. I try it out on a few things. It makes some different noises, but none of them are anything like a rumble.

'We're wasting our time,' I go.

'We ain't tried under the bed yet,' says Annie.

We both get down on our stomachs, but we can't see properly. So we crawl under. We feel about in the dust until I come upon a sheet of paper. I hold it out in the dim light to read it.

'It's a letter,' I go.

'Who from?'

'I don't know. Someone called "Blackie and Son Limited".'

'What's it say?'

'Hang on, hang on!'

I struggle to read the words, some of which are quite long. 'Hey, this is funny,' I go.

'What?'

'It's to . . . Maria Rose. Listen. "We look forward to reading your next book. If it sells as well as *Oh, no, It's Gassy Cooke!* we shall all be very happy." What's John doing with this under his—?'

'Something's sticking in me!' says Annie. She twists to one side and draws out what looks like a long metal pipe. Except it's fixed to something. She pulls it further. A wooden handle appears. And then . . . a trigger.

'Jason, it's a gun!'

I start to pull myself slowly away. Annie stays there, looking helpless, holding onto this huge lethal weapon. It's not a toy. It's the real thing.

Suddenly there's footsteps. The front door goes. We're well and truly trapped. We freeze like rabbits as the footsteps tramp through the house.

The basement door!

I start to pray. There's nothing else I can do. And then John walks in.

'What's going on?'

'Please,' I mumble. 'We lost our ball.'

'No, you didn't! Now, what's going on?'

John strides over to the desk and flings paper this way and that. We push the gun away.

'Have you read any of this?' he says.

'No, honest!'

'Come on, out of there!'

We crawl out from under the bed and stand in front of him with our heads bowed.

'Let's see your pockets,' he says.

We empty our pockets. When he's satisfied, John walks round behind us, takes a quick

look under the bed and pulls the bedspread down to cover the gap. He sees me watching and glares. 'Nosey, aren't you?' he says. 'How would you like it if I went through your room?'

'Wouldn't like it.'

'No, you wouldn't, would you?'

John walks back to his desk. He picks up his hammer and taps it into his hands. I give him a sad little look, trying to make him feel sorry for us. He stares just as coldly as before. 'I think I know what to do with you,' he says.

'We're very sorry,' says Annie.

John strokes his chin. Then he opens his desk drawer and puts the hammer away. 'I've got a punishment that'll just suit you,' he says.

'What's that?' I go, in a weedy little voice.

John picks up a dirty shirt, and slings it at me. 'You can tidy my room!' he says.

On Sunday morning I wake up to a loud knock on the door. Before I can even answer, John is in the room. I grab my bag and push it under the sheets. I don't want him going through my things for revenge.

'All right, keep your hat on!' says John. 'I'm

only bringing you these, Sunshine!'

He holds out a handful of envelopes. Annie wakes up, rubs her eyes, and takes the ones with her name on. We tear into them. They're birthday cards—one from John, one from Aunt May. The one from Aunt May says 'Happy Birthday Dear Jason, With Much Love from Your Great Aunt May'. The one from John says 'Cheers Mate from Your Uncle John'.

'Oh, thanks!' I go. I can't say I much cared about a card before, but I want to be John's friend. If he's got a knife and a gun, he can probably take anyone on. But if I'm his friend then maybe he won't do anything terrible.

Annie isn't so friendly. She's sure now that John is the escaped criminal in the basement.

'You can't have your presents yet,' says John. 'I've got some business to finish off first.'

He winks and walks out. Straight away, Annie jumps out of bed and starts getting dressed.

'What's up with you?' I ask her.

'I'm going to talk to Auntie,' she says.

'Why?'

'I'm going to ask her straight out. I'm going

to find out what's going to happen tonight.'

'You don't still think—?'

'Jason, he's got a gun! Just because he's acting friendly doesn't mean anything!'

I'm not going to let her drop us both in it. I get dressed as well and we both go downstairs, arguing under our breath. Annie raps on Aunt May's door. After the usual wait, Aunt May's face appears. She does look worried.

'Can I have a talk to you?' says Annie.

'Um . . .' says Aunt May. 'Well . . .'

'Only for a second.'

'Oh, well . . . I suppose if it won't take long—'

Aunt May stops. John has appeared in the corridor. As soon as he sees us he hurries along and stands between Annie and Aunt May.

'You know you've not got the time,' he says to Aunt May.

'Let us talk to her!' says Annie.

John turns on her. 'Here!' he says. 'Don't you snap at me! Your Aunt's busy today, so that's all there is to it.'

Annie looks at Aunt May. 'You'd better do as he says, dear,' says Aunt May. Then she closes the door. John waits till we've gone well away. He looks for all the world like a prison guard.

That afternoon I take him on. He opens the front door just as my football bounces that way, so he tucks it under his arm and tells me to try to get it. I punch at it but it's stuck fast and he laughs. Then I try twisting his arm but it's solid as a rock. I cheat by stamping on his foot but he just makes out he doesn't notice. I wonder if he doesn't have feelings like normal people.

At last he kicks the ball away, then when I go for it he wrestles me over. I cling on to his leg and try to bring him down. I'm just about to try my Japanese knee-twister when he looks up and rushes into the house.

Annie's at Aunt May's door.

'I told you to leave her alone!' says John.

I run up and grab him again, but he pushes me off, not laughing. 'You two had better get up to your room and stay there,' he says. 'I'll call you when it's dinner.'

Annie sits on her bed, watching the clock tick-tick-tick towards Sunday evening. I'm

angry with her. If she hadn't messed things up John would be in a good mood now and I would be on his side.

'What are we going to *do*?' says Annie.

'I was doing something,' I tell her.

'Yeah. Creeping round him.'

'I was not! I was getting him talking!'

'Liar! You're trying to make sure nothing happens to you. You just think of *yourself*.'

'Do not.'

'Do.'

'Do not.'

'And I'll tell you something else you can't face.'

'Oh, yeah?'

'You creep round him 'cos he's your *hero*!'

'No I don't!'

'Only babies have heroes.'

I leap over the bed and hold down Annie's arms 'Shut up!' I yell at her.

'See? You can't face it!'

'*Shut up!*'

Suddenly I lose control and smack her. She screams, then cries. At first I'm even more angry. Then I remember she's my sister, and we're stuck somewhere we don't even know, and it's our birthday, and we don't know what's going to happen to us. I feel sorry. I tell her. She still sulks. 'Just 'cos you're bigger than me!' she says.

'Tell you what,' I go, 'you can go and get John's gun, then we'll be even.'

'I don't want to *touch* his stupid gun!' says Annie, then suddenly clamps her hand to her mouth.

'What's up?' I ask her.

'Our fingerprints!' she goes. 'They're on the gun!'

'Maybe that's why we're here!' I go.

'What do you mean?'

I look into Annie's face, scared. 'We're going to take the blame,' I go. 'We're going to take the blame for what happens to Aunt May'.

When we're called to dinner, I slip my fossil stone into my pocket. We go down like two hunted animals, eyes and ears open.

Aunt May is in her usual place, at the far end of the table. She's wearing her best dress and a necklace of pearls, except they may be fakes. It's so hard to tell what's real.

The table's set for a special occasion. There's a lace tablecloth, and knives and forks which might be silver, and candles which send a flickering light over Aunt May's wrinkled face and sharp eyes. We sit down carefully amongst the cut-glass goblets and glinting blades.

The door to the kitchen swings open. John walks into the room with a half-smile on his face and a tray held high in the air. He lays it on the table. There's a bird on it, but not a chicken. John picks up his wicked carving knife and something which looks like a little

pole stuck onto a knife-handle. He slides the blade of the knife against the pole and it makes a squealing noise. The knife goes up and down the pole, over and over. He's sharpening it. When he takes it to the bird, it slices through the flesh as if the flesh were butter.

'Hold your pudding out for treacle!' he says, taking Annie's plate and half-filling it with slices of meat.

'What is it?' says Annie, nervously.

'Ostrich,' says John. Annie's face drops. 'No, only joking,' says John. 'It's a Lesser

Spotted Yodelling Mountain Dodo.'

'Don't listen to him, Annie,' says Aunt May. 'It's —'

'Ssh!' says John, putting a finger to his lips.

Aunt May shushes. The rest of the bird is shared out, and we help ourselves to the vegetables. But no one starts eating. We stare at the food like it's a piece of homework. I couldn't eat an aniseed ball.

'Something wrong with you lot?' says John, tucking in. I slice off a tiny piece of meat. Suddenly there's an almighty 'Aaagh!' My heart stops. I look straight up at Aunt May. The knife and fork have dropped out of her hands. She holds the side of her face. She's going purple. She's in agony.

'Shot!' she yells out. 'Oh, my heavens!'

Aunt May struggles to her feet. John puts down his knife but makes no other move. Suddenly Annie jumps up and rushes to help Aunt May.

'No, no, leave me!' says Aunt May.

Slowly, with a shaky hand, she reaches a finger and thumb into her mouth. She probes between her teeth. She brings out a tiny black

pellet, and holds it out in the palm of her hand.

'Look at that!' she says. 'Darn it!'

John shrugs. 'Sorry 'bout that!' he says. 'I was sure I'd got them all out.' He looks round at our open mouths and laughs. 'What's up with you two?' he says. 'It's only a bit of lead shot.'

'What's lead shot?' I peep.

'Lead shot? It's what you shoot the bird down with!'

'You mean you shot it?'

'Well, it didn't throw itself in the oven, did

it?' John laughs. He likes his own jokes.

'What if you swallow the shot?' says Annie.

'Well, you drop dead, don't you?' says John. 'Deadly poisonous, lead.'

'Take no notice,' says Aunt May, but we do all the same. I remember Mum threw away an old enamel saucepan because it had lead in it. I cut up my meat into tiny tiny pieces, scared stiff one of those little pellets will go down my throat. I mustn't stop concentrating for a second.

The meal ends in silence. John collects the plates.

'Now,' he says, 'special birthday treat. I'll tell you what, I'll even let you find it yourselves.'

'Where?' I go.

'In the fridge,' says John. 'You can take these plates out while you're at it.'

We do as he says. In the fridge we find four glass bowls of trifle, topped with cream and nuts and grated chocolate. Suddenly I'm sure everything's going to be all right. Of course nothing's going to happen to Aunt May! One look at those layers of jelly and sponge and

custard, and all my appetite comes flooding back.

We carry the trifles through. Annie keeps one and gives one to Aunt May. I keep one and give one to John. We're just going for our spoons when John says something's not right.

'This one's not for me,' he says. 'This one's for your aunt.'

Aunt May looks up in amazement.

'Why?' I go.

'We don't really want to go into that,' says John, 'do we, Aunt May?'

Aunt May mumbles without saying anything. I look at Annie. Annie's fingers shoot away from her bowl. Our fingerprints! On the trifles!

'Come on, Jason!' says John. 'Give Aunt May her trifle.'

He begins to look angry. I feel giddy. I stand up, walk round the table and find myself staring at the trifle, unable to move. Poison! Of course!

'Here', says John. 'Let me help you.' He grabs my hand and folds my fingers round the trifle bowl.

'There,' he says. 'That wasn't that hard, was it?'

He gives me a little push. I walk round to Aunt May like a robot, terrified. I place the trifle before her, and take her first bowl back to John, who pats me on the back and congratulates me.

'You're a mate, Jay,' he says. 'Aren't you?'

I look at Annie. She watches me, tensed up, like a frog about to jump.

'Dunno,' I mumble to John.

'Course you are,' he says.

Aunt May's mouth is open. She doesn't seem to understand anything. Absent-mindedly, she picks up her spoon.

'Why?' Annie suddenly blurts. 'Why's it for her?'

John smiles. 'Secret,' he says.

'I want to know!'

John looks at Aunt May. 'They are rude, aren't they, Aunt May?' he says.

'*Why?*' squeals Annie.

John leans across the table, folds his arms,

and looks Annie straight in the eyes. 'She's on a diet,' he says, in a loud whisper. 'She wants the trifle with no sherry.'

They stay there, staring at each other, in a battle of wits. Meanwhile Aunt May's spoon sinks slowly into the trifle and out again. I sit there, helpless, as she lifts the poison spoonful to her lips. Two inches . . . one inch . . .

'No!' screams Annie.

I leap up, smash my way straight over the top of the table and seize the spoon. Annie seizes the bowl. The front door slams behind us and we leg it down the road for all we're worth, still clinging onto the trifle. In no time the door slams again, and huge footsteps rain down behind us.

'Chuck it!' I yell. 'Chuck the trifle!'

'No!' yells Annie. 'He'll get it! He'll make us eat it!'

He's gaining.

'Down the front!' I scream.

We clatter down the hill towards the beach, in terror. For every two steps we take, John seems to take three. I spot a cut and skid round into it. Brambles fly up and hit us in the

face and hands. I see blood but don't feel pain. John arrives at one end as we duck out of the other.

Annie passes me the trifle. We race through the park and onto the promenade. It's black and wet and seems to stretch for a mile. Annie's wheezing and my dinner is jumping back into my throat. But we can't stop. My legs are like lead but we can't stop.

'The grass! Up on the grass!'

We scramble madly up the grassy hill where we found the fossils. John's shouting. He sounds no more than a few yards behind, with his great feet pounding the promenade. My feet skid and scrape and hardly seem to move forward at all. We reach the top of the grass hill, and suddenly realize we're trapped. In front of us is the jut of land with cliffs on all sides and the sea below. We run forward, hoping and praying for a miracle. Any second now John's shoulder will come thudding into the back of my legs.

'Now!' screams Annie. 'Sling it now!'

With every last ounce of strength I swing back my arm and chuck the trifle. It sails into the stars, bounces on a rock, and drops over the cliff edge and into a watery grave.

We leap round to face John. He's walking, quite slowly, over the grass, gradually penning us in. It's like being hunted by a giant shadow, maybe your own shadow.

Quietly, I pull the stone out of my pocket. John stops.

'Well,' he says. 'You two have really ruined

everything, haven't you?'

I move my arm back, ready.

'Do you know how long I've been planning this day?' says John.

I take aim.

John's head drops. 'Go on, go back to your aunt's house,' he says.

I put down the stone. John stays there, head down, looking fed up. 'Go on, go home,' he says again. We wait. It doesn't look like a trick. I move carefully forward and Annie follows. We creep past him, as far away as we can, but he doesn't move. Then we walk, faster and faster, looking back every two seconds. As we go down the grass hill and onto the promenade, no footsteps follow. He's given in. But we don't relax till we're well up the road to Aunt May's house.

'Why d'you think he let us go?' Annie asks.

'I don't know. It must be 'cos we got rid of the trifle.'

'I don't like it,' says Annie. 'It doesn't make sense.'

'I don't care. Mum'll be here soon.'

We reach the house. It seems very quiet. I

half expected to see police cars. We slump through the door, fall against the corridor wall, and feel safe at last.

'Aunt May?' says Annie.

No answer.

'Aunt May?' we both call.

No answer. We go into the dining room. Aunt May's chair is empty. I feel uneasy.

'Aunt May!' I shout again.

'Ssh!' says Annie. 'What's that?'

I listen. I hear Aunt May's voice. She's in her room. We rush to her door.

'Help!' we hear, dimly. 'The gas! The gas!'

'Oh, God!'

We rattle the handle. Locked. I yank it and force it and kick the door. Useless!

'Jason!' yells Annie. 'The French windows! Quick!'

We race out onto the front lawn. Annie tries the handles on the French windows. Locked again!

I think quickly. I spot my football on the rock garden. I race over, fetch it, and line it up in front of the windows. With one massive kick I send it smashing through the glass. In

seconds we've got our hands through and the windows unlocked. Then we're struggling with the curtains and tumbling wildly into the room. Where is she?

She's sitting in her armchair, completely unharmed, with her mouth open.

'Wh . . . wh . . . ?' she stammers.

Something drops out of her hand. It's a microphone. There's a tape recorder on the table in front of her. The gas fire is off and there's not the slightest smell of gas.

'Um . . . um . . . ' says Annie.

'Wh . . . wh . . .?' says Aunt May.

'I think there's been a mistake,' I go.

The curtains part. John walks through. 'Good God!' he says. He hurries over to Aunt May and puts a hand on her shoulder. 'Are you all right?' he says.

'They . . . came through the window!' murmurs Aunt May.

John picks up the football. He looks at us and shakes his head. 'Why?' he says.

'We heard her call for help,' I peep.

'Help?' says John. 'Does she look as if she needs help?'

'No,' I peep.

'What about my bowl?' Aunt May asks John.

'They threw it over the cliff!' says John.

'Over the cliff? My cut-glass bowl?'

'Don't ask me to explain it,' says John.

He sits down. So do we. There's a kind of stunned silence. Aunt May reaches down and switches off the tape recorder. Suddenly a thought strikes her. 'Oh, my goodness!' she says. 'I know what's happened!'

We're all ears.

'They've heard me talking into this silly thing,' says Aunt May, picking up the microphone.

John slaps a hand to his face. 'Of course!' he says.

It still doesn't make any sense to us.

'Shall I tell them or shall you?' says John to Aunt May.

'Go on,' says Aunt May.

John gets up, walks behind Aunt May, and puts a hand on each of her shoulders. 'Twins,' he says, 'Meet Maria Rose!'

'What?' I go.

'The writer?' says Annie.

'You've got it!' says John. He points to the tape recorder. 'And this is how she writes. Thinks up her story, then speaks it all onto tape. Doesn't believe in using a pen. Easy, isn't it, Aunt May?'

'Not with those two creeping round all night,' says Aunt May, nodding at us.

'But why didn't you tell us?' says Annie.

'That,' says Aunt May, 'would have spoiled your little surprise,'

Aunt May reaches under her chair and brings out two home-made books. She hands one to each of us. 'Happy birthday, twins!' she says.

I look at my book. It's called *Jason and Annie to the Rescue*. Inside, neatly typed, is a whole story with Annie and me as the main characters. So that's what she's been doing all week!

'Aren't you pleased?' says Aunt May.

'Yes! Yes, thanks!'

'How about a kiss for your auntie, then?'

We both give Aunt May a kiss. Her eyes wrinkle up with pleasure. 'That's all the thanks I need,' she says.

'Don't I get any thanks, then?' says John.
Annie frowns. 'What for?' she says.
'Who d'you think typed it?'
'You?'
'You know it was me! You heard the typewriter, didn't you?'
'The rumbling!' says Annie.
'Eh?'
'We never knew what it was!'
'Well, you know now, don't you?'
Suddenly everything fits. I feel a real idiot. We say thanks to John. He doesn't really know how to take it, just nods his head. I look down

at the broken glass, and think of Aunt May's trifle bowl sailing over the cliff. I say how sorry I am. Aunt May tucks one of us under each arm and gets very serious.

'Listen,' she says. 'They're just Things. Things don't matter. *You* are what matters. And don't let anyone tell you different.'

By the time Mum arrives we've cleared up the glass and read our stories. Mum looks dead happy and healthy, and she's got all her work done. She even went out one night. She gives us such a cuddle I don't know where to put myself.

'Had an accident with the ball, Mum!' I go.

'Jason!' says Mum. 'After all I've told you!'

'Don't worry,' says Aunt May. 'It's been a pleasure having them. They've given me a whole new lease of life. Such lively imaginations!'

We pack our things and put on our coats. Mum thanks Aunt May over and over again for giving us a birthday we won't forget. She says she knows we enjoyed ourselves because we never even remembered to ring her.

'Oh yes!' says Annie. 'We did, Mum! But someone else answered!'

'Did you get the number right?' says Mum.

'Course! Five three two two eight!'

'And the code? Did you remember the code?'

'The what?' we go.

'Well, you've got to dial a code as well if you're not in Bristol.'

Mum looks at our faces and laughs. 'Come on,' she says. 'We've got a train to catch.'

We troop out of the front door, ready to say our last goodbye to Aunt May's house. John doesn't like saying goodbyes too much. He waves and disappears into the basement. I'm quite sorry. I might even write him a letter and tell him to stop killing birds.

Aunt May kisses us goodbye.

'You must just tell me one thing,' she says.

'What?' says Annie.

'Why exactly *did* you throw my trifle over the cliff?'

'Um . . . ' says Annie.

'We just . . . thought John was trying to poison you!' I tell her.

Aunt May laughs and laughs and laughs. 'Such imaginations!' she says, drying her eyes. 'John wouldn't hurt anybody! After all,' she adds, with a twinkle in her eye, 'he doesn't want to end up in jail again, does he?'